D1516760

Game On

Have You Got What It Takes to Be a Video Game Developer?

by Lisa Thompson

Compass Point Books ✦ Minneapolis, Minnesota

First American edition published in 2009 by
Compass Point Books
151 Good Counsel Drive
P.O. Box 669
Mankato, MN 56002-0669

Editor: Marissa Bolte
Designer: Ashlee Suker
Art Director: LuAnn Ascheman-Adams
Creative Director: Joe Ewest
Editorial Director: Nick Healy
Managing Editor: Catherine Neitge
Content Adviser: Christian Bradley, Academic Director,
        Game Art and Design and Video and Game Programming,
        The Art Institute of California, San Diego

 This book was manufactured with paper containing
at least 10 percent post-consumer waste.

Library of Congress Cataloging-in-Publication Data
Thompson, Lisa, 1969–
    Game on : have you got what it takes to be a video game developer? /
by Lisa Thompson. — 1st American Ed.
        p. cm. — (On the job)
    Includes index.
    ISBN 978-0-7565-4208-5 (library binding)
    1. Video games—Design—Vocational guidance—Juvenile literature.
    2. Video games industry—Vocational guidance—Juvenile literature.
I. Title. II. Series.
    GV1469.3.T46 2010
    794.8—dc22   2009014862

Image Credits: BigStockPhoto.com, 21 (t), 39 (b); Bedo, 42 (m); ciajd, 8 (t); diomedes66, 21 (golden mace); Egorkat, 21 (spear); grybaz, 41 (m); Kamaga, 16 (m); Natael, 21 (sword); Neo Edmund, 32 (t); njnightsky, 22 (b); phildate, 5 (b); photoclicks, 20 (t,bl); rgbspace, 44-45 (bkgrnd); Scott Hancock, 35 (t); sean gladwell, 23 (t); SlidePix, 9 (m); Stockagogo, 48 (t); Surpasspro, 42 (t); VHVisions, 4-5 (bkgrnd); wingnutdesigns, 23 (b); Dreamstime.com/Algol, 11 (t); A-papantoniou, 45 (m); Bertrandb, 46 (tr); Digital-studios, 20-21 (bkgrnd), 32 (m); Fat*fa*tin, 3 (bl); Felker, 26 (t); Heros, 44 (t); Homeriscool, 10 (t); Jaymast, 6-7 (bkgrnd; Kentoh, 10-11 (bkgrnd), 38-39 (bkgrnd); Kts, 13 (b); Ladykassie, 7 (t); Leeloomultipass, 36 (m); Mcseem, 47 (t); Migutas, 30 (m); Milosluz, 38 (t); Patrick, 33 (t); Pixac, 12-13 (bkgrnd; Prawny, 22-23 (bkgrnd), 24-25 (bkgrnd); Redbaron, 6 (b); Ronfromyork, 3 (tmr); Sergydv, 12 (b), 35 (m); Smithesmith, 25 (m - Wii); Stillfx, 16-17 (bkgrnd), 46 (b); Svidenovic,, 10 (b); Thorsten, 26-27 (bkgrnd); Vling, 27 (t); Yuris, 45 (t); Fotolia, 31 (t); Beboy, 33 (b); chris jewiss, 34 (b); Christopher Howey, 8 (bl); feisty, 15 (m), 47 (m); Igor Dutina, 40-41 (bkgrnd); imageZebra, 30 (bl); KiWiE, cover (l), 17 (b); Michael Smirnoff, 36 (t); Ralf Bürkle, 31 (m); Ralf Kraft, 20 (br), 21 (m –all, b-all), 34 (t), 39 (m); Robert Spriggs, 38 (b); iStockphoto/adamfilip, 5 (t), 46 (tl);

Alija, 33 (m); alwyncooper, 36 (b); Atropat, 28-29(bkgrnd); browndogstudios, 44 (mr); caracterdesign, 17 (t); cherokee-jones, 7 (b); Dreef, 26 (m); Duncan1890, 1; enot-poloskun, 18-19 (bkgrnd); fpm, 3 (br); goldhafen, 16 (t); gummy231, 3 (tl); Inok, 15 (t); kencameron, 37 (t); lisapics, 8 (br); Lobsterclaws, 29; lolong, 39 (t); madisonwi, 48 (b); Marcus-Photo, 42 (b); mstay, 30 (mr); mwookie, 44 (ml); Nicolas_, 6 (t); norgen, 6 (m); Pannonia, 8-9 (bkgrnd); peregrina, 3 (m-green game control); prill, 14-15 (bkgrnd); qavondo, 28 (t); Rellas, 42-43 (bkgrnd); rosen_dukov, 37 (m); scottdun-lap, 3 (bm); serdarduran, 13 (t); slobo, 43 (m); Spectral-Design, 12 (t); ssuni, 3 (tr); tepic, 4 (t); track5, cover (r), 3 (tml), 4 (b), 9 (t), 26, (b), 27 (ml, b), 40 (b); urbancow, 43 (t); VikramRaghuvanshi, 41 (m); vm, 9 (b); YinYang, 18 (b); Shutterstock/Emelyanov, 32–33 (bkgrnd); Jason duckworth, 28; jaymast, 30-31 (bkgrnd); Maugli, 14; Perov Stanislav, 40 (t); sgrigor, 18 (t); Sony Computer Entertainment Australia, 24 (b), 25 (m,b)
All other images are from one of the following royalty-free sources: Big Stock Photo, Dreamstime.com, iStockphoto, Photo Objects, Photos.com, and Shutterstock. Every effort has been made to contact copyright holders of any material reproduced in this book. Any omission will be rectified in subsequent printings if notice is given to the publishers.

Visit Compass Point Books on the Internet at *www.compasspointbooks.com*
or e-mail your request to *custserv@compasspointbooks.com*

Table of Contents

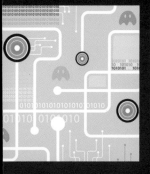

Games, Games, and More Games

Everywhere I look, I am surrounded by games. My corner of the office is covered with game design books, game demos, cover art, and proposals that my team and I are working on.

As a game developer, I am thinking, writing, playing, or talking about games most of the day. While finished games can be a lot of fun, getting there involves hard work and long hours!

My latest project is pretty exciting. We are developing a new game called *Level 11*. It is still in the early stages, but I'm excited about the direction the game is taking. I've got a busy time ahead of me over the next few months.

PUN FUN

Will this video game system last five years? Obsoletely!

What does a game developer do?

A game developer is a person who makes video games. Developers create the concept, layout, and game design. Game developers decide the goal of the game, the rules of play, and the look of the game. They decide what it's about and how it looks and sounds—so pretty much everything related to the game is up to them.

Every game developer dreams of coming up with a game that explores new areas and is original and compelling.

Game on

Digital and electronic games can be played on:

- computers

- televisions with attached game consoles, such as Sony PlayStations, Microsoft Xboxes, and Nintendo Wiis

- hand-held game consoles, such as Nintendo's DS, Sony's PSP, and Apple's iPod touch

- personal digital assistants (PDAs) and other hand-held computers

- cell phones

- arcade machines

Game consoles are popular now.

People can play games on their PDAs.

5

Skills Needed to Be a Game Developer

- excellent computer skills
- wide knowledge and understanding of video games
- creativity and imagination
- problem-solving skills
- patience and attention to detail
- flexibility and adaptability
- good teamwork and communication skills
- ability to work under pressure and meet deadlines
- willingness to keep up with industry developments

rough draft

Ideas go from my notepad to my computer.

Skill up

Being a game developer involves lots of writing, so it is important to have as much writing experience as possible. Graphic design and programming skills help developers to understand visual and technical possibilities and to discover new areas to explore.

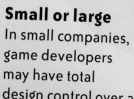

Small or large

In small companies, game developers may have total design control over a project. In larger companies, new developers may work on just one aspect or level of a game and work under a head designer.

Here, there, and everywhere

Over the past several decades, video games have become a huge part of our culture. Video games are now a multi-billion-dollar industry. Successful games often inspire related merchandise, such as toys or T-shirts.

Movies into games into movies

In the past, successful movies have inspired their own games, such as *The Chronicles of Riddick*. That still happens, but now successful games, such as *Tomb Raider* or *Silent Hill*, are made into movies.

When games go bad

In 1982 Atari released a video game based on the movie *E.T.: The Extra-Terrestrial* for the Atari 2600. It is considered to be the worst video game ever and was a huge flop. Rumor has it that Atari buried thousands of the unsold game cartridges in a New Mexico desert landfill.

There's no guarantee a game will sell.

How I Became a Game Developer

I caught the game bug young.

I have always played games for fun. While in college, I studied computer science, and I made my first game for an assignment. I had a group of friends who liked playing games, and that's pretty much all we would talk about. I was either playing games or looking at books on how to design games.

I got a part-time job testing games for a development company near the university. There wasn't a lot of money involved, but I hoped the experience would lead somewhere. Eventually it did. One day while I was in my final year of study, they were really busy and asked me to write some copy for an educational game they were working on.

This is where I work.

After that my boss invited me to sit in on some development meetings when they were fleshing out game ideas. I enjoyed coming up with new ideas and trying to invent new styles of gameplay.

When I finished college, I was hired as a full-time employee, and I have been with them for three years now. I guess my best piece of advice for anyone who really wants to work in the games industry is play, play, play, and try to build on and improve the games you enjoy. You never know—you might come up with a totally new and highly addictive game—every game developer's dream!

In meetings I listened carefully, then tried to bring new ideas to the table.

Culture vultures

Video games are so popular now that gamers have their own culture. They discuss games and share tips in online forums and in virtual communities. Many colleges even have gaming social clubs.

What Is a Game?

Games are rule-based, interactive environments. They often involve challenge or conflict, and are designed to have a defined outcome. Video games can be divided into five main categories.

stealth game

1. Action games
- arcade shooting games, such as *Duck Hunt* or *Space Invaders*
- first-person and third-person shooters, such as *Counter-Strike* or *Halo*
- stealth games, such as *Metal Gear* or *Tenchu*
- dancing games, such as *Dance Dance Revolution*
- action-adventure games, such as *The Legend of Zelda*
- platform games, such as *Mario* or *Sonic the Hedgehog*

2. Strategy and war games
- real-time strategy and tactics games, such as *World of Warcraft* or *Halo Wars*
- turn-based strategy and tactics games, such as *Sid Meier's Civilization* or *Final Fantasy Tactics*
- management games, such as *SimCity*, in which players are rulers of their own world

3. Simulations
- sports simulations, such as the *Madden* or *NCAA* series
- vehicle simulations, including driving games, such as *Gran Turismo* or *Crazy Taxi*

4. Role-playing games
- turn-based, role-playing games, such as the *Final Fantasy* series
- massively multiplayer role-playing games, such as *EverQuest* or *Guild Wars*

5. Adventure games
- text-based adventures, such as *Avalon*
- graphic adventures, such as *Torin's Passage*

Top 5 game genres

1. First-person shooters
Players see the action through the eyes of their characters. The goal is simple—fire at anything that moves.

2. Real-time strategies
The key to these games is usually balancing defense and attack. They offer the player more than one way of approaching each battle. These games require the ability to plan and predict consequences.

3. Sports games
These games follow the rules of real-life sports, such as football or snowboarding.

4. Puzzles
Problem-solving skills are needed for these games, such as *Minesweeper* or *Bejeweled*.

5. Role-playing games
Players take on the role of an adventurer and go on a series of quests that lead to the story's conclusion.

11

Game Design

The process of game design can be broken down into individual steps.

Step **1** **Imagine a game**

- What is the big idea or high concept?
- What is your game about?
- What type of game is it—action-adventure, mystery, role-playing, etc.?
- What are the goals for the player?

Step **2** **How will the game work?**

- What are the rules of the game?
- How will it become more difficult as the player progresses?
- What will end the game?

Step **3** **Describe the game**

- What is the setting?
- How many characters does it have?
- What special features will it contain?
- What will it look like?

Documenting the design

- What is the blueprint for the game's development?

A blueprint is a set of guidelines that defines all the rules of the game. They are written by the game developer for the team to follow. It is the developer's role to produce a clear and comprehensive guide to the game.

The game idea

Ideas for games come from four main sources:

- original ideas—brand new ideas of possible worlds, characters, and stories

- other media—films, TV, books, music, popular culture

- other games—improving on existing games and adding to popular games

- the real world—games inspired by life

We're only limited by our imaginations.

Pac-Man champ

On June 5, 2007, 10 people from eight countries played in the first *Pac-Man* World Championship in New York City. Daniel Borrego of Mexico became the first *Pac-Man* world champion and won an Xbox 360 console. It was specially decorated with *Pac-Man* artwork and signed by the creator of *Pac-Man*, Toru Iwatani.

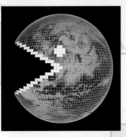

13

Elements of Game Design

One of the first questions a game developer needs to ask when designing a new game is "What is the goal of the game?"

Possible goals

- save something or someone, such as a princess locked in a tower

- find something, such as an ancient or lost treasure

- play as long as possible to achieve the highest score

- successfully finish a series of levels

- defeat other players or characters

First outline the basics of the game:

- the goal of the game

- the game's intended audience

- the genre of the game

- the game's unique selling points

PUN FUN

When my PlayStation was stolen, my family was there to console me.

Once the goal of the game is understood, there are three key building areas of the game that need to be addressed:

1. rules
2. story
3. interaction

1. Rules

All games are formed on a formal set of rules. Rules can come in various categories, including:

- rules that limit player action
- rules that are clear and easy to understand
- rules that apply to all players
- rules that are fixed
- rules that are binding
- rules that are repeatable

The rules of any game can be divided into three types.

Constitutive rules are the mathematical rules of a game. These rules are the building blocks of the game—for example, the sky will always be blue or each character will have four eyes.

Operational (explicit) rules are the rules of play that players must follow when playing the game. These rules are the actual rules of how to play. For example, you have to take turns, or you can only jump using certain items.

Implicit rules are the unwritten rules of good and fair behavior. They should be understood when a game is played, so players don't use rude or aggressive language.

2. Story

The story is what drives the game. The story contributes to the look, feel, and pace of the game.

Game plots can be as simple as jumping obstacles to get to the other side of a river, or as difficult as following multiplayer narratives.

Simple or complex, for the game to work, the story must both persuade players to play the game and hold their attention once they're playing. Games must also have a variety of obstacles and outcomes to keep the player interested.

Puzzles and story intertwine in most games. Imagine a maze is blocking the player from the castle. The player must navigate the maze before entering the castle and continuing the story. And there's your game.

The *World of Warcraft*

The *World of Warcraft* is the world's largest MMORPG—massively multiplayer online role-playing game. More than 11.5 million players subscribe to the online game. Blizzard Entertainment launched the first *WoW* game in 2004, selling 240,000 copies on its release date. The expansion pack, *Wrath of the Lich King*, released in 2008, sold more than 2.8 million copies on its first day and another 1.2 million that month, making it the fastest-selling computer game of all time.

Testing, testing

Name: Emma Dunne

Occupation: Game tester

Basically I play games all day, pushing them to their limits—and beyond. My job is not as easy as you might think. I have to find bugs in a game, and then reproduce them. I backtrack every step I've taken and try to narrow it down to the essential things that trigger the bug.

Problem-solving and deduction abilities are crucial to being able to quickly find a bug and then report it to the programmer or developer so we can figure out how to fix it.

If you want to be a tester, you have to really love playing video games, because you might be playing the same game every day for months. To get it right, you might be playing the same level of the same game for weeks. The trick is to find new ways to approach the game so you don't get bored.

The worst part of the job is when you end up tracking a single bug for hours on end. You might want to give up, but you have to keep going. Game testing requires lots of patience and can be tedious.

③ Interaction

Developers need to ask themselves a series of questions about how the player will interact with the game, such as:

- What kind of player is the game aimed at?

- What will the game look and sound like?

- Is the game in the first person or third person?

- Does the player assume the role of the main character?

- Is the game for a single player or for more than one? If it's a multiplayer game, how do the players interact with each other?

- What is the heart of the gameplay—speed, action, or style? Is the game continuous or turn-based?

- How much control will the player have?

Challenges, gameplay, and victory

Gameplay refers to how exciting or interesting a game is to players. It is also used to describe the amount of time it takes to finish an entire game.

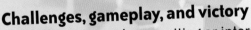

Challenges are the elements of the game that force the player to play the game and solve puzzles in a new or different way. Developers need to think about the number and complexity of challenges for each level.

Developers may also want to incorporate minigames, short games contained within the bigger game. They provide different challenges in a game and a break from the main story.

Once a level has been created, it is continually tested by game testers. A game tester will play a section of the game over and over, trying many ways to move through the level. He or she will take notes of all the potential problems in the game. Game testers will play a game until all aspects of it are perfect.

Most games have a special kind of rule that defines victory—when a player has won the game—but not all games can be won. Shaping victory and loss is an important part of successful game design.

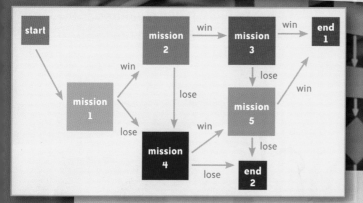

A decision tree is a diagram that maps out all the possible decisions and outcomes in a game. It helps developers understand how players move through the game and the possible endings.

What is *Level 11*?

Level 11 is a first-person combat-based game. It is a doorway into 11 layered worlds of monsters. Each level is a different environment containing a particular monster that must be found and defeated. Each monster can only be defeated with a particular piece of weaponry that players also have to find.

As the player progresses through the game, each level becomes more and more dangerous as monsters from previous levels appear and the environments become increasingly complex. Players must use multiple combat skills to survive.

For me, this is one of the most exciting parts of developing a game—choosing among all the possibilities. I'm imagining how all the levels will look, the sound of the creatures as they roar, and how to make the game interesting and fun to play. We've designed some great monsters.

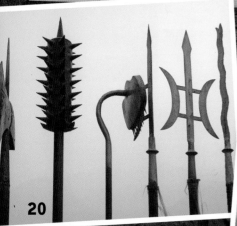

basilisk

LEVEL	MONSTER	WEAPON
1	hellhound	Durendal sword
2	golem	Cernwennan dagger
3	troll	Gáe Bulg spear
4	ghoul	Sudar disc
5	demon	Mjolnir hammer
6	centaur	Zeus' thunderbolt
7	griffin	golden mace
8	minotaur	Fragarach sword
9	basilisk	fire javelin
10	gorgon	Gandiva bow
11	kraken	Kusanagi sword

Cernwennan dagger

golden mace

Fragarach sword

Gáe Bulg spear

centaur

demon

griffin

troll

21

A History of Video Games

It is important for game developers to have a good understanding of the history of video game design and key moments in gaming evolution.

1958
Physicist William Higinbotham invents the first video game in New York—a tennislike game played on a machine called an oscilloscope

1962
First interactive computer game, *Spacewar*, is created by university student Steve Russell

Higinbotham's game was called Tennis for Two.

1970
Nolan Bushnell and Ted Dabney create an arcade version of *Spacewar* called *Computer Space*—the first video arcade game

1972
Bushnell and Dabney start the Atari company

1975
Atari releases 150,000 home consoles of the arcade game *Pong*; even with its $100 price tag, *Pong* becomes the hottest Christmas present that year; people wait in line at stores for hours—not to buy the game, but to put their names on a waiting list

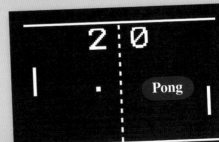

Pong

1976
Space Invaders, the first game to track and display high scores, appears at arcades

1977
Atari launches the first cartridge-based home computer system, the Atari 2600; games can now be bought separately and played using the console and a TV set

an original
Atari 2600

1980
The first 3-D arcade game, *Battlezone*, is created by Atari; set on a virtual battlefield, it is used by the U.S. government for training exercises

The arcade game *Pac-Man* is released worldwide by Namco; an alternative to space shooter arcade games, it becomes one of the most famous games of all time

Defender, the first arcade game using a virtual world, is introduced

1981
Nintendo reveals the arcade game *Donkey Kong*, the first platform game, which allows players to jump over obstacles and gaps

The arcade game *Dragon's Lair* is released—the first game to feature laser disc technology

Laser discs were much larger than CDs or minidiscs.

1985

The popular puzzle game *Tetris* is developed by Russian programmer Alex Pajitnov; originally played on computers, today *Tetris* is available in almost every format, including PDAs and cell phones

Most games between the 1970s and 1990s were on cartridges

Nintendo releases the Nintendo Entertainment System (NES), known as the Famicom in Asia

1986

Nintendo releases the hand-held Game Boy

1991

Nintendo releases the Super NES

original Game Boy

1993

The computer game *Doom* is launched; it has groundbreaking graphics and networked multiplayer gaming

1994

In Japan the Sega Saturn and the Sony PlayStation both hit the market

1995

PlayStation becomes the most popular game console, with 20 million sold

first Playstation console

1996

Nintendo begins selling the Nintendo 64 in Japan

The Tamagotchi virtual pet becomes an instant sensation, with more than 70 million sold

2000

Maxis releases *The Sims*; it becomes the best-selling PC game ever; with no defined goals, players create virtual people and control their lives and environments

Sony releases the PlayStation 2

2001

Microsoft and Nintendo introduce their next-generation systems—the Microsoft Xbox and the Nintendo GameCube

2004

The Sony PSP (PlayStation Portable) and the Nintendo DS go on sale

2005

Microsoft releases the Xbox 360, which allows players to compete online and download games, trailers, TV shows, and movies

2006

The Nintendo Wii is launched; its wireless controller is made up of the "Wiimote" and "nunchuck"

Sony releases the PlayStation 3

2009

With more than 40 million units sold, Nintendo's *Wii Sports* becomes the best-selling video game of all time; the previous record holder was another Nintendo game: *Super Mario Bros.*

Who's Who on the Game-Building Team

Development teams vary according to the size of a company and the game being produced. Our company is quite small, but we still have members of the team who perform specialized roles.

Game programmers

Game programmers are responsible for the game as a whole. They look at the big picture and are responsible for setting deadlines for coordination and marketing. The game programmer works closely with the producer to set realistic targets and make sure the team meets them.

Lead programmer and programming team

The lead programmer heads up a team of programmers in creating the tools for the art and sound. They develop the game's structure, which is the basis for the game's functions, graphics, and sound.

Game developers

Developers are often programmers who create the computer code to make each game. They may have other responsibilities, such as managing other team members or working on whole games in smaller companies.

Artists

In our team, each artist has a specialized role in character, texture, or background creation. They create the look of the game.

Level designers

Level or "mission" designers build the structure of the game and fill it with objects, goals, and enemies. They work with me as well as with the programmers and artists.

Writers

Writers work closely with the developers to work on the story and dialogue. They also write any tutorials and other text that may accompany the game.

Sound designers

Sound designers are responsible for any and all sounds that occur in the game. Since sounds create mood, character, and atmosphere, the designers need to be able to create their own sounds, as well as use sound libraries and other sources.

Developing Communication

As a game developer, it's my job to have a clear vision of what the game will be like when it's finished. That's why my job is most intense at the preproduction stage, making sure the teams are on target from the start.

Game developers rarely create a game alone. Documenting the game's design and keeping the team aware of changes is crucial. It is very important to have constant communication with other sections of the development team.

Doom

Released in 1993, the game *Doom* kick-started the first-person shooter genre. An estimated 10 million people downloaded it within two years. Its lifelike environment, sounds, and new perspective changed the look and feel of gaming. Some have even heralded it as the greatest video game of all time.

The game was so addictive that some players suffered *Doom*-induced motion sickness (also referred to as *Doom* sickness or DIMS). They would vomit after spending hours at their computer screen, while other people even passed out.

The Father of modern gaming

Nintendo was founded in Japan in 1889 as a playing card company. In the early 1950s, the company even made cards for Walt Disney featuring his popular characters. In the 1960s, the company's toy division became successful. The company also began producing video games.

A student product developer named Shigeru Miyamoto was hired in 1977 to work on one of Nintendo's first coin-operated arcade games, *Radar Scope*. After the game flopped, Miyamoto reused the hardware and created the first *Donkey Kong* game. The game's hero, Jumpman (later known as Mario), soon became the company's mascot. He has appeared in more than 100 games on a dozen gaming platfoms.

Miyamoto went on to develop some of Nintendo's best games, including *The Legend of Zelda*, *Star Fox*, *F-Zero*, *Pikmin*, and *Nintendogs*.

PUN FUN Some video game equipment was shot. It was a graphic display.

My job includes making sure everyone understands the game's intended look, feel, and function. The team must communicate well to make changes and deal with problems quickly and effectively.

It's about getting everyone moving in the right direction.

A good developer has a broad understanding of the areas involved in creating the game. He or she must understand the possible problems and offer suggestions and solutions.

Often big changes to a game need to happen, and it is the developer's job to explain the changes and the reasons behind them to the team. Game design is as much about communicating ideas as it is about coming up with them.

Designing the Settings and Characters

Getting an idea for the look of a game is often vital for success.

At the very early concept stage, artists often work with the developer and come up with sketches for environments and characters. Storyboarding is a useful way to work out how the characters will move through a world.

> We considered having a dragon in the game ... then decided against it.

storyboard

Artists also come up with a range of colors, tones, and moods for the game. The visual feel can define a game just as much as the control system or level layout.

Seeing is believing

A game's environment is extremely important. Effects such as reflections, shadows, surface shine, and cloud patterns all contribute to making an environment appear more convincing.

It can be tricky to make clouds look real.

As we throw around ideas for *Level 11*, all ideas and suggestions are documented. People share their thoughts about the game and where they are with their part of the project.

The artists present some rough sketches for the monster characters, settings, and perspective. The writers discuss dialogue for various levels, and the sound designers play sounds they think will create a unique atmosphere.

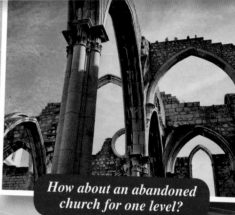

How about an abandoned church for one level?

We set to work on producing a demo of the game, and the producer and I discuss deadlines for various stages of the project.

In the zone

Games need to be challenging enough so that they do not bore players, but not so challenging that players get frustrated. It's not easy to find the right balance so players will enjoy the game and its challenges.

Gaming Special Features

Easter eggs

Some games contain secret, hidden messages, images, or locations known as Easter eggs. The first Easter egg was created about 30 years ago. Easter eggs are now a standard part of most games.

In the beginning, gamers stumbled across random keystrokes or mouse clicks that made a secret animation appear or a hidden room accessible. Now there are Web sites to help gamers discover these special features.

If you push the second and fourth levers down, what happens?

Who knew that secret chamber was there?

Hidden eggs

The first game to have an Easter egg was the 1979 game *Adventure* for the Atari 2600. By collecting a hidden dot, players could enter a hidden room where the words "Created by Warren Robinett" (the game's inventor) would appear on the wall.

Cheat codes

Cheat codes are button combinations or control sequences that allow players to advance to a hidden level or perform moves that cannot be blocked.

Get some unbeatable ninja moves.

Modifications

Modifications are enhancements or additions made to a game. Mods can be new tools, characters, settings, levels, music, or story lines. Mods can be made by the developer or the computer-savvy public. Mods add to the success and life of the game by adding interest and extending the replay value of the game.

More *Doom*

Doom was one of the first games to gain a large gaming community interested in creating modifications. The ability to create custom levels and modify the game was an important aspect to the game's original appeal and success.

Level Design

A level designer is responsible for creating each level's own game world—building the environment, placing every object, and deciding its purpose. The level designer decides the enemy's route, how fast he or she moves, and the best places to pick up things such as time bonuses or extra items or lives. They make sure players never hit an unintended dead end.

This level has a cool spaceship.

These designers must create hidden paths to coax players through the world—without the players realizing it.

Creating moods and feelings

Level designers must also create the feelings of suspense, anticipation, and victory in a game. Players should often feel as if they're about to run out of time or supplies, but rarely fall short completely.

Designers learn how to place packs, item reserves, or checkpoints just within reach, but far enough away so the players are bracing themselves for "Game Over." A smart level designer tweaks, tries, and tweaks again until the game has the right mix of surprise, thrills, and victory.

Pacing

Level designers control a game's pace so that it is not too boring or slow, but also not too intense all the time. Games need to have calmer moments, then build up to excitement—such as in racing games, where designers must leave surprises on the track but also keep the rhythm of the course.

Adventure

In third-person adventure games, the designer places visual clues to show players which parts of the level they can reach to keep them interested and playing the game.

Worldwide knowledge

The best game developers have a broad range of interests and knowledge in:

- mathematics
- logic
- history
- literature
- art
- science
- current affairs

35

The Characters Come to Life

Progress meeting with the art and production team

Rough sketches are finalized and scanned into computers where they become controllable 3-D characters. The designers then begin to bring the characters to life by defining the characters' shape with control points. These control points will guide the movement of the character when it is in motion.

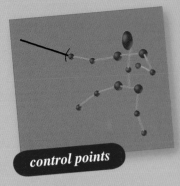

control points

Next the designers add skin, colors, and surface texture to the character. Finally the programmers and designers work together to give the character the ability to move.

Our troll needs to look real.

The game's character can move now.

For superrealistic movement, human actors are filmed wearing special suits with sensors that represent the control points of the character's skeleton. These movements are then transferred to the animated character.

Progress meeting with the sound team

Games can require hundreds of individual sound effects. Since there are 11 monsters in *Level 11*, we ask the sound designer to provide samples for each monster to inspire the art team.

voice artist at work

The sound designer also needs to build different sounds for each level. Gamers understand the power of music. When the music stops, they know they are in trouble.

Each monster needs a variety of sounds, such as when disturbed, surprised, angry, and fighting. The sound team and I talk about how we will create some of the stranger monster sounds. We'll need to get creative!

fading out the music

Talk the talk

Gamers have developed their own vocabulary.

Leet   (also known as l33t) written language using keyboard characters to communicate over the Internet

noob   (also known as newbie or n00b) someone who is new to gaming and asks silly questions with obvious answers

über   biggest and most powerful

pwn   to have outplayed someone else in a game (as in, "You just got pwned!")

Design Documentation

Now that we have a clear understanding of the goals, gameplay, look, and feel of the game, it is time to lock it all into one design document. This book is a map of the project for everyone on the team.

While there is no single structure for game design documents, some things are always included.

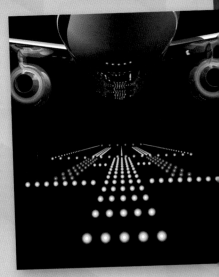

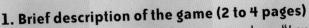

1. **Brief description of the game (2 to 4 pages)**
   The most basic ideas of the game, such as, "*Level 11* is a third-person shooter game in which players must find a specific weapon to kill a monster on each of the 11 levels."

2. **Game treatment (10 to 20 pages)**
   A treatment is a broad outline that lists the basic ideas and aspects of gameplay. It addresses things such as:

   - what is the planned perspective—first person or third person?

   - what is the structure—levels, chapters, challenges?

   - what is the heart of the gameplay—speed, action, puzzles?

   - will there be a multi-player function?

   - how difficult is the game?

   - how long will it take the average player to complete?

3. In-depth game description (50 to 200 pages)

This is a detailed account of how the game will work. It covers all creative and technical aspects of the game, such as:

- who is the player's character?

- list of the characters in the game and a description of their personalities, capabilities, and how they act

- how the various levels are set up

- detailed structure of the game

- full description of the style of the graphics, outlining the mood, tone, and palette

This could be you in the game.

choosing the environment

Wild West setting

Testing and Tweaking

As we develop the game, it is tried out by game testers who search for bugs and glitches. Developers must expect to make changes and learn how to compromise without sacrificing the quality of the game.

Testers play each level, pushing the game as far as they can. They identify bugs and glitches that need to be fixed.

Bugs range from minor art glitches to major crash bugs. They can be divided into four categories:

- **A-class bugs**—cause the game to crash or lock up. This category also includes bugs that cause installation failure or keep features from working

- **B-class bugs**—include graphic glitches such as scenery pop-up or frame-rate issues

- **C-class bugs**—spelling errors or minor graphic and audio glitches

- **D-class bugs**—usually minor suggestions, such as an unappealing color scheme or texture

Stages of the debugging process

1. identify program behavior as a bug
2. report the bug to the developers
3. developer analyzes the bug and fixes it
4. developer verifies the bug is fixed
5. regression testing—game tester retests the game to make sure the bug has not reappeared

The test and tweak cycle

Testers first receive an alpha version of a game. It is quite basic and is only tested for major flaws.

The next test version is beta. It is tested by a larger group. The game is tested more thoroughly for bugs and flaws. Countless cycles of testing and fixing go on until developers are satisfied the game is ready for public release.

PUN FUN After punching his computer and breaking his hand, he needed tech knuckle support.

Marketing

Games are a multi-million-dollar business. A big, blockbuster game can cost between $3 million to $5 million to develop and an additional $10 million to promote and market.

High-tech sales talks are popular now.

The promotion and marketing of a game begins while the game is still being designed. Publishers try to create as much hype as possible about a game before its release. Developers and public relations staffers are sent to trade shows and conventions worldwide to get the word out about the game and generate interest.

Hong Kong's convention center

Promotional versions of the game, known as demos, are sometimes made available as downloads from the Internet or as bonus features on other games before the general release. These sneak peeks, plus Internet and TV trailers, help to build hype. It is hoped they will increase market interest and ultimately increase sales of the game.

PUN FUN The video game designer had a dog whose bark was worse than its byte.

The marketing team plans a game release.

Level 11 is released

Finally the game is finished and launched. It's monster madness. Posters and demos are everywhere. Some people have already found the secret levels. You can buy it off the Internet or in stores.

If *Level 11* succeeds, there may be talk among the production team about doing more *Level* games. I'm already jotting down ideas and thinking about improved gaming strategies and challenges.

That's the life of a game developer—you never stop playing the game.

There's a pro for everything

In 2007 the Major League of Gaming hosted 208 teams (16 professional teams, 16 semipro teams, and 176 amateur teams) for its 4-on-4 *Halo 2* tournament. The prize for the winning team was $20,000 (split between the four team members.) The MLG National Championship that year awarded more than $475,000 in cash prizes.

The MLG has around a dozen players under contract, with the best players making more than $250,000 over three years. However, sucess is short-lived—MLG co-founder Mike Sepso doubts that most players have the ability to remain competitive after the age of 30.

Follow These Steps to Become a Video Game Developer

Step 1

Finish school with the best grades possible, especially in English and math. Study art, design, and computer technology if you can.

Step 2

Enroll at a college or university that specializes in technical fields such as game development, computer science, digital media, or animation.

Step 3

Play as many games as you can. Study games you like and think about why you like playing them. Think about their strengths and weaknesses. Invent new rules. Brainstorm ideas with friends.

Gaming experience is a must

Are you a collector?

In 2009 Japanese retailer Mandrake offered a complete collection of all 1,051 Famicom games (known as the NES in the United States). The collection, which cost 650,000 yen (U.S.$6,700), included all Famicom games released in Japan between 1983 and 1994.

Find inspiration on the Internet. Check out sites with simple games like *Space Invaders* and download their files to study how they are built. Create your own mod or small game. This shows employers you are motivated and teaches you important skills about problem solving and the development process.

It's never too early to start.

Keep trying and don't give up. Practicing your skills can only make you a better designer, programmer, and writer. Your first ideas may be based on your favorite games, but keep at it and you will become more and more original.

Read industry magazines, attend gaming conferences, and keep up-to-date with blogs that developers keep on the Internet.

Opportunities for game developers

The computer games industry is growing and there are many game-related careers available, such as:

- **IT project management**—developing business computer systems

- **Web designing**—creating and maintaining Web pages

- **multimedia development**—working with images, sound, and text to create multimedia programs for clients

- **animation**—bringing drawings and models to life on screen

45

Find Out More

In the Know

- Video games are expected to surpass movie box-office revenues in the future. Video games are the fastest-growing segment of the entertainment industry.
- More than 145 million Americans play computer and video games. One-third of all Americans say that video games are the most fun form of entertainment.
- Nearly 40 percent of game players are female. In fact women over the age of 18 represent more than 30 percent of the game-playing population, while boys age 17 and younger make up only 20 percent.
- As of 2007, the Game Industry Salary Survey estimated that the average salary for a game developer was around $66,000. The average salary for all levels of programmers was $80,000.

Further Reading

Cohen, Judith Love. *You Can Be a Woman Video Game Producer*. Marina del Rey, Calif.: Cascade Pass, 2005.

Cunningham, Kevin. *Video Game Designer*. Ann Arbor, Mich.: Cherry Lake Publishing, 2009.

Trueit, Trudi Strain. *Video Gaming*. Ann Arbor, Mich.: Cherry Lake Publishing, 2009.

Internet Sites

FactHound offers a safe, fun way to find Internet sites related to this book. All of the sites on FactHound have been researched by our staff.

Here's all you do:

Visit www.facthound.com

FactHound will fetch the best sites for you!

Glossary

arcade game—coin-operated game often found in restaurants and video game arcades; commonly fast-paced games that require hand-eye coordination, such as pinball or shooting games

constitutive rules—mathematical rules of a game that create the gaming experience

Easter eggs—special features, including secret messages, special images, or the revealing of locations

first-person—game where all action is seen from the eyes of the main character

game cartridge—removable piece of software that contains instant access to media as well as some ability to save information

gameplay—player's overall experience while playing a particular game

graphic design—designing print and visual media for video games, advertisements, magazines, and more

implicit rules—unwritten rules of gaming etiquette that should be understood by all players

Leet—alphabet used by online gamers

MMORPG—massively multiplayer online role-playing game; computer game in which a large number of players take on the role of a fictional character and interact with other people in a virtual environment

operational rules—rules that players must follow while playing the game; also known as explicit rules.

platform game—game in which players jump on and off platforms and over obstacles

role playing game (RPG)—game in which the players assume the form of fictional game characters

storyboard—sketches showing how a game's characters and how the plot will progress throughout the game

third-person—game where the main character is seen on-screen at all times

Index

Look for More Books in This Series: